Christian Perspectives
on Theological Anthropology

Christian Perspectives on Theological Anthropology

A Faith and Order Study Document

Faith and Order Paper 199

World Council of Churches, Geneva

Cover design: Rob Lucas

ISBN 2-8254-1457-3

Printed in France

Table of Contents

Background

1. The understanding of human nature is a decisive factor in analysing, and addressing, many of the sensitive issues facing the churches and the ecumenical movement today. Additionally, traditional Christian understandings of human nature, its origin, limits and possibilities, seem increasingly under threat due both to societal challenges facing humanity today and to developments in the natural sciences.

2. This Faith and Order study programme on Theological Anthropology was carried out in response to requests made at the WCC Harare assembly, and in the years following, for work on theological anthropology as a contribution to the churches' reflection in this area. The study aims to help the churches address vital issues and situations where the understanding of human nature is challenged. It is understood as a contribution to the churches' common reflection, witness and service, and as a resource for their work on certain theological and anthropological issues which continue to divide them. Results from the study process include "Ten Common Affirmations on Theological Anthropology" which are offered as a basis for the churches' common reflection. These are printed individually throughout the text and then brought together at the end (§127, and the inside back cover). In addition there is an "Invitation to the Churches" and questions to encourage local use of the study document (§§128-129).

3. The study is not intended to develop a comprehensive systematic Christian anthropology. It seeks rather to do something more modest: for the sake of the unity of the church, and in an accessible way, to reflect on complex and sensitive issues related to a Christian understanding of human nature so as:

(1) To pay close attention to selected challenges which face humanity today;

(2) To articulate what the churches can say together about what it means to be a human being;

(3) To name differences in the churches' understanding of human nature which impair the churches' common confession, witness and service;

(4) To encourage the churches in working together on the spiritual, ethical and material challenges facing humanity today.

Nor is the document which has been produced an ecumenical consensus text. It rather records the results of a study process and is offered, as such, to the churches and interested parties for their use in addressing these issues. A brief basic bibliography is also included.

4. In this text, the experience of Christians in situations where human life is under threat or question is explicated in engagement with Scripture and Tradition. The text arose from a process in which Christians from diverse traditions strove together to forge a theological statement that should be faithful to that experience, as well as to the historic sources of Christian understanding. On this basis the text comes, in its conclusion, to a number of common affirmations as noted above. These affirmations are offered as an invitation to the churches to work together in deepening theological reflection and common action towards life abundant for all human beings.

5. The study process included two planning meetings (in Brighton, Massachusetts, USA [2000], and Belfast, Northern Ireland, 2001); two major consultations (in Jerusalem, 2002, and near El Paso, Texas, USA, 2003); and two drafting meetings (in Montevideo, Uruguay, 2004, and in Geneva, Switzerland, 2005) which produced the present text. The locations of the main consultations were chosen intentionally as places where humanity is under challenge.

6. The process which led to the text could not have been possible without the hospitality and generosity of many, many people, including all those who hosted the meetings, those who shared their stories and those who contributed written papers and documents. Where the text is rich, it is a result of their bounty.

Introduction

A. THEOLOGICAL ANTHROPOLOGY

7. From the very beginning of the Church, Christians have grappled with the issue of what it means to be human in the light of the gospel. Drawing on the rich resources of Scripture and Tradition, they have developed distinctive understandings of human beings, their relationships and their achievements. These understandings constitute what is called "theological anthropology", i.e. a theologically informed view of humanity (from the Greek anthropos, human being).

8. Through history the development of this theological anthropology has taken place in dialogue with ideas about humanity found in the broader culture of the time. There are wide areas of general agreement in which people with different perspectives can share common insights, learn from one another and make common cause. There are areas where the Christian voice is distinct from other voices. At the same time, Christian theological anthropology is not concerned only with Christians, but is committed to all humanity, with its diversity of culture, colour, gender, sexuality and beliefs. Christians offer insights into the human condition which they believe are true for everyone and which, in fact, affirm the equal worth of all and celebrate human diversity.

9. Theological anthropology is also in many cases deeply challenging to social structures that demean human beings. It sets its face resolutely against all that disgraces or destroys human beings created by God in God's own image. Christians of diverse traditions have joined in supporting human rights around the world against all that treats people as no more than tools or instruments for the purpose or profit of others.

10. In a world where views of humanity may veer between confident optimism and utter cynicism, Christians believe that human beings, societies and cultures, have all the potential for creativity, responsibility and goodness that comes from being made by God, and yet are deeply affected by sin and brokenness. Sin denies the worth and dignity of human beings, disrupts community and hampers the flow of love and justice. Sin must be faced, confessed, forgiven and healed.

For Christians believe in costly reconciliation and love, not an easy and unreal optimism.

> *Affirmation:* **All human beings are created in the image of God and Jesus Christ is the one in whom true humanity is perfectly realized.**

11. The question, "What are human beings that you are mindful of them, mortals that you care for them?" (Ps. 8:4) has troubled people almost since time began. It is a question that has reverberated down the ages and will not go away. It is one with which we dare not cease to contend. Yet it is a question which allows of no facile or simplistic answers. The human person is complex and lives in an ambiguous world: this affects every assertion we make about human life. But, more than that, human beings are, properly speaking, "mysterious", i.e. imbued with something of the sacred mystery which comes from the Spirit or breath of the infinite Creator. The insights which Christian understanding gives into this mystery of what it is to be human have the depth not of complex and abstract theories but of truths grasped by faith in the midst of life, suffering and joy.

12. One vital key to the mystery and reality of human beings which Christian Tradition offers is this: human beings are made in the image of God. The reflective work of this study has been animated by this wonderful and profound belief. In the pages that follow this belief is probed and interrogated, affirmed and expounded. The life-situations recounted in Part I of this study – which tell of challenges to the actuality and understanding of what it is to be human – drive us to a more searching exploration of this belief. At the same time, the many-layered truth of this biblical and historic belief has shown itself able to speak powerfully to these situations of challenge.

13. Many Christians and Christian communities work in the cause of human wellbeing without knowing anything explicitly about "theological anthropology". They did not necessarily have to wait for the theology to be expounded before speaking the prophetic word God gave them or performing God's work. However, there is a special need, when Christians work together, to support their common witness and fortify their common endeavour by giving an account of the shared

faith which underlies that witness and work. This account not only aims to express the shared faith of the churches, but also to model the way in which that conviction about human nature engages with, and responds to, the urgent cries of the world.

B. METHOD

14. The mandate for this study, issued in Harare at the close of the 8th Assembly of the WCC, called for reflection on theological anthropology through the lens of contemporary contexts and experiences. Study consultations were therefore held in places where people were struggling with complex realities, for example, in Belfast, where the ongoing "troubles" have a clear religious dimension; in Jerusalem, the Holy City for Christians, Muslims and Jews, but today the focus of spirals of vengeance in the ongoing struggle between Israelis and Palestinians; near El Paso, on the frontier between Third World poverty and the affluence of the United States; and in Montevideo, a city which suffers deeply from the effects of the economic "meltdown" that affects so much of Latin America.

15. In each venue consultation participants were inspired and challenged by what was heard, and became especially attentive to those whose lives have been devastated by dehumanising forces. Courage and hope were found to be nurtured in places where many are driven to despair. It is humbling to listen to people involved in ministry and service in such situations, where the wholeness of human life seems almost impossible. Sometimes a contemporary version of the roll call of the heroes of faith listed in Heb. 11:4-38 was recounted. Often the challenging words "they, without us, shall not be made perfect" (v. 40) rang out. Amid all there has been a vivid awareness of the surrounding "great cloud of witnesses" (12:1) to encourage continuing discipleship in various contexts.

16. Those working on the study have paid attention to the contexts in which they have met so as to hear, in these contexts, what God is saying to them and to the broader Church. They have also attempted to bring these contexts into dialogue with the Bible and with Christian theology, to point towards a serious and relevant contemporary theological anthropology.

I. Contemporary Challenges

17. While throughout history the worth and dignity of the human person have been under threat, the current context in which human beings live presents a number of contemporary challenges. These call for a re-examination of what it means to affirm the humanity of all people. Today, the effects of ethnic and economic globalisation have changed both the way people live and the way in which people are treated in the Northern as well as in the Southern hemisphere. Unlike earlier times, we no longer live in closed, isolated communities relatively ignorant of, and unaffected by, what occurs in other parts of the world. Instantaneous communication and a global economy mean that what happens thousands of miles away almost immediately impacts local communities and the persons who make them up. The obsession with ever-increasing profits by multinational companies has immense consequences for those in so-called "developed" as well as in so-called "developing" countries with employees – as well as goods – often being treated as commodities.

18. These and similar realities of contemporary society not only result in very visible manifestations of a broken world, such as acute forms of poverty, increased violence and suffering, but also accentuate new challenges to humanity posed, for example, by pandemics such as HIV/AIDS. The conflicts arising all over the world through ethnic, cultural and religious differences now affect us immediately, if not physically then emotionally through the barrage of television images and the graphic photographs of the print media. The manipulation of genes, cloning, and developments in artificial intelligence (AI), raise brand new questions about the beginning and end of life and, indeed, about the nature of human life itself.

19. Obviously – as in the case of biomedical research – not all contemporary challenges are threats to human existence or to theological anthropology. Many challenges are in fact opportunities full of promise for new ways of being and of understanding ourselves to be persons of worth and dignity created in the image of God.

20. As has been pointed out already, Christians are not the only ones who seek to grapple with anthropological issues arising from the con-

temporary challenges which impact humanity and our understanding of human nature. Sociologists, economists, psychologists, ethicists, anthropologists and many other specialists, of other faiths or no faith, bring to bear significant insights on the human condition and the nature of humanity. For the Christian community, however, it is crucial that these challenges be reflected upon theologically in order to gain fresh insights on theological anthropology relevant and applicable to our new global context. Given this global context, it is especially fitting that this theological reflection be undertaken ecumenically.

21. Employing an inductive method, those pursuing this study have reflected theologically on specific instances of contemporary human experience which challenge our understanding of what it means to be human beings, made in the image of God. As a result, they have come to a number of common theological insights about what it is to be human. In this section of the report no attempt has been made to describe, or even list, all the contemporary challenges which impact humanity and theological anthropology. Instead, three illustrative sets of related challenges are grouped together. These groups of challenges arose out of the personal experiences and situations of those who participated in this study. Other, or additional, challenges will present themselves in each local situation, and the churches in each place will need to address these together on the basis of their common faith convictions.

> *Affirmation:* **All human beings, though created in the image of God, are inevitably affected by individual and corporate sin.**

A. BROKENNESS

22. We live in the midst of a broken world where faces and forces of threatened human worth and dignity abound. Here are sketched some of these faces and forces, which were made flesh by those who came together at consultations in this study.

1. *Violence*

23. The prevalence of violence poses serious challenges to the traditional understanding of humanity in the image of God. Indeed violence pervades our world. The Middle East, where persons met for one consultation, is but one among many instances of the crushing daily reality of violent actions and images invading our lives today. Near the southern border of the United States of America, where persons met for another study consultation, the issue of illegal immigration is a pressing topic. Those who gathered became aware of the complexity of this problem, and the suffering of the poor and desperate who are exploited as they seek a better life for themselves and their families.

24. Due to rapid urbanisation, global economic changes, and the impact of mass communication, the social fabric of societies is being eroded. Participants in the study heard, for example, from Brazil where educational and income inequalities are among the highest in the world. There these forces have led to the increase of violence among youth in a society where masculinity is built on values of aggression. All this is exacerbated by an increase in the use of drugs and criminality.

25. Sexual exploitation is a global problem. Participants heard from Thailand where the sexual exploitation of women and children is one of the country's burning issues. Many young women from rural areas are lured to the cities with promises of work in the factories, or as domestic servants. On arrival they are forced into prostitution. Although prostitution is a legal offence, many officials "turn a blind eye" because there is a very real link between prostitution and tourism, the military, and transnational companies. When tourism becomes an integral part of a country's economic structures, it is not surprising that there is a lack of enthusiasm for searching for viable alternative occupations for those engaged as sex workers. Generally these young women are driven by economic necessity, as they live in conditions of extreme poverty and are ruthlessly exploited. This is a prime example of the way women tend to bear the burden of double exploitation.

Patricia is only 18. She went abroad to work as a hotel reception-
ist, but when she arrived there the job did not exist. She was
forced to work as a prostitute. When "they" knew that she was
HIV positive, they sent her back to her own country. She is receiv-
ing treatment, but cannot get a job. She is happy that she was not
murdered by those who tricked her. She never speaks about her
experiences abroad. She is a very sad woman. (Uruguay).

26. The pervasive presence of violence in today's world challenges us as Christians to ask serious theological questions about our under-standing of human nature. What is the origin of this violence? Is it the result of sin and of the alienation of human beings from their true identity as beings created in the image of God? Is it the result of a distorted understanding, and misuse, of power? Is it caused by see-ing others, especially the weak and vulnerable, as somehow less than human, and thus fit "objects" for exploitation? Or is it the result of an inability, even on the part of professing Christians, to love selfless-ly, as Christ loved?

"In January 2003 I had to give up the lecture on the ecumenical
events of the previous years which, for over twenty-five years, I
have been presenting annually on the occasion of the unity week.
This was because of the curfew that was imposed on Bethlehem,
even though it was Christmas day for the Armenian Church and
Epiphany for the Eastern and Oriental Churches in Jerusalem.
Where is the image of God, with its glory, in the midst of all this?
What is the image that the soldier at the checkpoint projects on
the Palestinians who queue up daily in front of him, in order to try
to get to their work, their school, their hospital, their mosque or
their church? They seem patient externally, but are often boiling,
so angry inside, because of the continuous absurd loss of time
and frightening humiliations, and because they are being prevent-
ed from nourishing their families or procuring the necessary care

*for their sick. And what about the Palestinian desperate
kamikaze who causes his own explosion in the middle of a crowd
of Israeli civilians on a bus or in the market place? What image
does he nurture of himself as well as of the persons he intends
to kill or to hurt? These are only a few of the questions that kept
haunting my prayers". (Frans Bouwen, Jerusalem)nurture of himself as well as of the persons he intends to kill or to hurt? These
are only a few of the questions that kept haunting my prayers".
(Frans Bouwen, Jerusalem)*

2. *Poverty*

27. Whenever people are understood as commodities, and where money is understood as determining human identity and human worth, there are serious implications and consequences for our common Christian understanding of theological anthropology.

> *Affirmation:* **Sin can pervert or dis-
> tort, but cannot finally destroy,
> what it means to be human.**

28. Economic injustice causes dreadful poverty in many parts of the developing world. Some people are reduced to living in conditions not worthy of human beings, while others prosper. Slavery – while condemned by the churches and officially by most societies – continues in other, often hidden, forms. Global market economies are thrust on societies that are not geared for them. Global economic systems disrupt traditional societies, displacing economic and educational infrastructures. The market demands of such systems make access to prevention and treatment of disease difficult and expensive. It is ironic that international organisations such as UNAIDS and the United Nations call on countries to restructure their spending to ensure that "national budgets are reallocated towards HIV prevention", when these very countries are often hamstrung by crippling foreign debt.

29. Sometimes, young people drift into a meaningless exile in pursuit of spiritual or material satisfaction, caught up in the desire for meaning and purpose but unsure where to seek them. There is a new epidemic of estrangement of people from each other and from God, an epidemic brought about by poverty, and structural adjustment programmes are designed to meet the requirements of the developed world rather than of those whose need is the greatest.

30. On the other hand, we are also acutely aware of the threats to the image of God in those who enjoy material prosperity, disproportionate privilege and power. These things can diminish, and even mar, the image of God in us by encouraging the delusion of self-sufficiency, possibly resulting in the breakdown of authentic relationality and community.

31. It is important to distinguish among three types of poverty, each with important implications for how we understand human beings and human society. First, "holy poverty" is poverty chosen for Christian reasons and taking very seriously Jesus' statements that the poor are blessed, and that disciples should give up their possessions and follow him. Those who embrace holy poverty do so in solidarity with the poor. Their life-style, identifying as it does with the poor, witnesses to the value in God's eyes of those who are commonly despised and face all sorts of hardships because of their poverty. Holy poverty is simultaneously a protest against valuing people in terms of their material possessions, and an affirmation that those who are poor in material possessions are of infinite value in the eyes of God.

32. Secondly, "absolute poverty" is the condition of not having sufficient resources to provide for food, clothing and shelter – the basic necessities of life. Those in absolute poverty are destitute, not knowing where the next meal will come from, lacking shelter, nourishment and security, living on the edge of starvation. In today's world, in fact, tens of thousands of children die of starvation each day while multitudes more walk in hunger and despair. In Brasil, the poverty of some and the greed of others have even led to the tragic sale of children's organs. Absolute poverty is dehumanising and tends to destroy community and to set one person over against another. (We recognise, however, that a joyful sense of community and sharing is sometimes

to be found in the most awful slums and shanty-towns; saints can flourish in squalor and need.)

33. Thirdly, "relative poverty" identifies a situation in which there is a wide gulf of inequality between the rich and the poor, with the poor and marginalised excluded from the normal facilities and expectations of their society. Poor people and communities in the US and Europe are not badly off when compared with slum dwellers in Sao Paulo or Chennai; but, when compared with their own fellow citizens, they are severely disadvantaged. In such situations the ties of community are weakened. Crime rates tend to be high; the rich sometimes retire to "gated communities", providing for their own security and sanitation while the poor are left to fend for themselves. This extreme inequality within rich nations mirrors the extreme inequality between rich and poor nations.

34. Poverty, both absolute and relative, is a major theological challenge and practical problem facing Christians today, demeaning human beings and obstructing the neighbourly and loving relationships we are called to enjoy. In both cases Christians should support economic and social policies which affirm the equal worth before God of all who bear God's image, remembering that the just distribution of material things – food, clothing, shelter – is charged with spiritual significance. Alternate domestic, national and global responses to poverty are difficult to find; but Christians should never lose the hope of finding better ways of sharing and enjoying together the resources God has given, and of affirming the worth of human beings created in the image of God, irrespective of their physical circumstances.

3. HIV/AIDS

35. Any attempt to think about theological anthropology and human suffering in the context of HIV/AIDS must take into account profound ethical questions about human sexuality and relationships between women and men. In particular, Southern Africa is at the epicentre of an HIV/AIDS pandemic bringing untold suffering and death to millions. In that region, between six and seven hundred thousand people die annually and approximately 1,500 new infections occur daily. If the pandemic continues unchecked, ten million South

Africans will have died of AIDS-related diseases by 2010, two million children will be orphaned and the average person will not live to age forty. Southern Africa, however, is not the only region affected by HIV/AIDS. The sub-continent of India, and even wealthy countries such as the USA, have huge numbers of affected people – many of whom do not even know their condition.

36. Probing beyond the statistics it appears that women's vulnerability to HIV/AIDS occurs on a variety of levels: biological, social, individual, maternal and care-giving. For instance, an HIV-positive pregnant woman runs the risk of transmitting the virus to her child, either during pregnancy, during birth, or after birth through breast feeding. Rural women, who have little or no education and who live in traditional patriarchal relationships, have scant access to information on HIV/AIDS and in general lack the skills and power needed "to negotiate safer sex".

37. HIV/AIDS presents a number of significant challenges to theological anthropology. At least in some circles the condition has raised again questions (often uncomfortable or "inappropriate") about the connection between disease, sin, and the fallenness of humankind. HIV/AIDS has also highlighted, in stark reality, the interrelationship of individuals and community – both human and Christian.

38. The Body of Christ needs help in finding its way through the present ravages of sickness and death caused by HIV/AIDS. Attending funerals every weekend is a numbing task; it is more than numbing when the Church, as the Body of Christ, itself feels amputated as its members fill coffins. There are no dividing lines between the Body and some other reality "out there": we too are infected. Through HIV/AIDS we learn, in a new way, that when part of the community suffers, the whole community suffers (1 Cor. 11:26). In this sense it could even be said that "the church today has AIDS".

Sergio said: "I had been in prison for three years when I was tested. I was only 20. Then another prisoner told me - Welcome to the club, you are HIV positive! I did not know anything about the virus. I did not listen to him. I did not say anything to my family, but little by little I became sick and weak. First my skin, then my lungs, my stomach. I did not receive any treatment, because the resources of the national health programme are not used to save the lives of delinquents. I am scared, waiting for death." Sergio died two years later. When the family knew of his illness and his death, they did not want to bury him. The church community buried him. (Uruguay)

Sinethemba said: "I am 33 years old and come from Butterworth where I live in a small shack with my sister, my cousin and a friend. In 1997 when I was pregnant, I was diagnosed HIV positive. My child was not healthy for a single day." Sinethemba, whose name means "we have hope", died in 1998. After Sinethemba died, my husband chased me away from my home because of HIV/AIDS. He did not like the idea that we might be positive. I asked him to come with me to the hospital for a test, and he was HIV negative. I had terrible diarrhoea; my body was covered with a terrible rash. My immune system was collapsing. Last July I started on anti-retrovirals and my problems are gone. I am surprised that the president says these drugs are toxic. I cannot agree because they have given me my life.   (Tembi, South Africa)

B. DISABILITY

39. Another challenge to theological anthropology comes from the reality of human disability. We began with more general reflections on a Christian understanding of human identity and value. Against this background we turned to the specific issue of disability, developing our reflection in encounter and dialogue with disabled persons themselves.

1. Identity and the challenge of diversity

40. "O Lord, how manifold are your works! In wisdom you have made them all; the earth is full of your creatures" (Ps. 104:24). The psalmist sings praise to the Creator for creation's rich diversity of which human beings are a part. We, too, sing praise to God for the gift of

creation, of life, and of the diversity that is intrinsic to us as human beings made in the image of God.

41. There are many different – and different kinds of – human identity markers: among others ethnicity, race, caste, national belonging, religious identification, gender and sexuality. Identity is developed in interaction with other persons, within the various social contexts (family, church, school, work, ethnic group, nation) in which one lives. (See also the Faith and Order study on ethnic identity, national identity, and the search for the unity of the church.)

42. A crucial insight of the Christian faith is that all such identity markers are as nothing beside our new identity in Christ (Gal. 3:28): that no human identity markers, however positive and precious, can deny our primal belonging to Christ; and that no human distinctions, however pervasive and pernicious, can be allowed to separate us from our sisters and brothers in Christ.

43. But human beings often live in ways that do not express their true identity as created in the image of God. They may deny the gift of relationality, and fear and reject the gift of diversity. The longing to be "at home" and secure carries within it the potential for the exclusion of others. Ethnic or national identities may be maintained through opposing, or even demonising, other groups. We acknowledge that most of us are taught to fear the other, the stranger, the alien. Worse, we have crafted mechanisms (walls, cf. Eph. 2) to distance and dehumanise the other. In such cases diversity becomes divisive, often with catastrophic results.

2. Disability and the norm of "perfection"

44. The fact of human disability challenges our understanding of humanity as made in the image of God in special ways. Among other things it exposes the unconscious assumption, which pervades many of our cultures, that only a "perfect" person can reflect fully the image of God – where "perfect" means to be successful, attractive, young and not disabled. In the gospel, Jesus Christ calls us to be perfect in love, even as our Father in heaven is perfect. He offers us a different kind of image of perfection, one about giving things away rather than acquiring them: "sell all that you have and follow me". In his

Kingdom the smallest and last are first, and we must love both our neighbours and our enemies (Mt. 5:43-48, 10:42, 19:30). It is also, as we shall develop later, a perfection made manifest in weakness and suffering.

45. This is not the kind of image made in the media, by image makers, but the image that we are called to see when we look in the mirror, and in the faces of those around us. The fullness of this image is expressed through life in human community. To be created in the image of God is to be of infinite worth, an infinite worth which is shared by every human person whatever their physical or mental condition.

3. Disability: an embodied perspective

46. How can these affirmations be developed in relation to disabilities? The following paragraphs represent one attempt to do so, and in a way which reflects the experience of disabled persons themselves.

47. Reflection on the body is helpful for a theological anthropology that attends to disability, because the body is the source of our knowledge not only of ourselves but of the world and everything in it. An emphasis upon the body is a development of constructivist epistemology, in which human knowledge is regarded as a human creation. Human knowledge is created by humans. Human knowledge takes the form of constructs, which express the social and political position of the knower. The emphasis upon bodily knowledge takes this further by pointing out that we know the world as our bodies know it: the body is an epistemic principle. (See also the Faith and Order study on ethnic identity, national identity, and the search for the unity of the church).

48. This is particularly important for a philosophy and a theology of disability because it enables us to postulate the existence of several worlds of human knowledge. The experience which a blind person has of the world is so significantly different from that of sighted people that we can speak of it as a "constructed" world. This emphasises the independence and integrity, the wholeness of the blind world, and sets blindness free from being interpreted merely in terms of deficiency. Blindness is not just something that happens to one's eyes; it is something that happens to one's world.

49. This enables us to also relativise the hegemenous assumptions of sighted people, who do not always realise that they live in a world which is a projection of their sighted bodies, but make the mistake of thinking that the world is just like that, the way they see it. Such people are never able to respect or understand blind people, but will always regard them as being merely excluded from the sighted world, and not as having a more or less independent world of their own.

50. The significance of this for theological anthropology lies in the fact that it emphasises the plurality of human worlds, and the recognition of the plurality immediately relativises the absolute claims of a single, dominant world. There are many kinds of human bodies, some young, some old, some male, others female, some with arms and legs, others without arms or legs, some who hear, others who do not hear, some who are rich and others who are poor, some who oppress others and some who are oppressed. This enables us to make a further distinction between the human worlds which are "natural" in that they spring from the body as natural body-knowledge, and those worlds which are the social constructions of power and greed. When we recognise natural epistemic worlds, we can also recognise unnatural ones. It is true that the rich and poor know different worlds, but this is an epistemic distinction stemming from injustice; it is also true that the blind and the sighted know different worlds, but this is an epistemic distinction which should be recognised and honoured.

51. We see then that a theological anthropology must begin by emphasising the relativising impact of plurality. Only when this is done, can the experiences of disabled people be understood and respected as making a positive contribution to the fullness of human life, and only when this is done can the artificial divisions between human worlds be recognised for what they are – the disembodied shadows of evil which settle upon and oppress human bodies. For it is the affirmation of one category of world that makes possible the denunciation of another category.

52. When we think of the body of Christ we discover a theology of disability which is supported by various elements within the Christian faith. These include the implications of the fraction, i.e. the breaking of bread by the priest at the eucharist, and the scarred and wounded

body of Christ the King. The first of these symbols reminds us that brokenness lies at the heart of the paschal mystery and that the church is united through brokenness. The second symbol reminds us that the Christian story, while it converges upon the perfection of a liberated cosmos, does not conform to the images of perfection which are found in our present culture, but witnesses to a range of patterns of perfection. At this point we encounter the Christian paradox of strength through weakness and life through death. The perfection of God is a perfection of vulnerability and of openness to pain. Part of the mission of the church is to bear witness to the God of life by accepting many forms of human life and by sharing in human vulnerability and pain. In this respect, part of the mission of disabled people is to become apostles of inclusion, witnesses of vulnerability and partners in pain.

C. NEW TECHNOLOGIES

53. A further challenge to theological anthropology comes from two areas in which, in different ways, radical questions are being put to traditional understandings of what it means to be human. The first of these areas is emerging biomedical technologies. These promise many advances in the quality of human life, but at the same time pose bafflingly complex questions to society as a whole and, not least, to Christian faith: At what cost, and to what other forms of human life, do these benefits come? Who shall receive them? What are the long-term implications of genetic manipulation, and can we even foresee them in their fullness? Who decides, and who decides who decides? What are the implications for our understanding of humanity's role within creation, of human uniqueness, of human nature as created in the image of God – and, indeed, for our understanding of God?

54. The second area is that of artificial intelligence (AI) research. AI offers great benefits to humanity, but poses formidable social, philosophical and religious questions: What are the possible costs? What are the implications for society, for example for the role and dignity of work? Who shall reap the benefits? Again, who decides, and who decides who decides? What are the implications for our understanding of human intelligence – and human uniqueness as created in the image of God?

55. Biomedical technology and AI research, which seem at first sight to be disparate disciplines, present both common challenges to our understanding of the human person as made in the image of God. Theological language is entering the public debate in both these areas: biomedical research is said to be "playing God" in the creation of new life, and AI research is said to be replicating the human reasoning process, which has traditionally been closely associated with what makes us uniquely human.

56. In the history of the human family, of course, the development of new technologies is not new. New tools make possible new ways of being in the world and new possibilities for the flourishing of human community (for example, the history of human agriculture is marked by the development of plants and animals that meet specific human needs, through the careful selection of specific desirable traits, such as longevity, hardiness and productivity).

57. The human creativity called upon by these disciplines is a God-given gift; and recent developments of new technologies in these fields have great potential benefits for the human community. Yet the application of the inherent human capacities for innovation and adaptive selection may, through some of the technological innovations available or under development, be creating a new situation with unprecedented possibilities for the manipulation of human nature. Such developments challenge the whole human community and all of creation. Issues of justice are also at stake: the development and dispersal of highly sophisticated technology in a world where many do not have access to the most basic of material resources needed for human well-being is always a matter for Christian consideration.

58. On the basis of input from experts in the fields of genetics and AI, we wrestled with the implications of such new technologies for our understanding of what it means to be human, made in the image of God, and explored some of the ethical issues confronting humanity in these areas today. The issues are complex and technical; indeed experts, too, may differ in their interpretation of certain data and in their ethical argumentation and conclusions. This underscores the importance of clarifying the basic parameters of the discussion: the technological options presently available and under development; the

ethical principles from which one is arguing; and the material and ethical consequences of each possible course of action.

59. The instances we consider here (necessarily in a very concentrated way) serve both as particular cases, with particular cause for interest and concern among Christians; and as general examples, showing how an ethical analysis should clarify the possible courses of action, and the ethical implications of each.

1. Developments in genetics: implications and options

60. Many novel ethical issues have arisen from recent rapid development in genetics. Their ethical assessment is highly dependent on our view of the status of the early embryo.

(a) The early embryo

61. Up to fourteen days after conception, an embryo consists of "stem cells", entities that are capable eventually of development into all possible types of tissue, but which are not yet so differentiated to generate any structures. Is such an early embryo already fully human, or only potentially so? Christians have taken two contrasting positions: a) the embryo has the full moral status of a person from its conception; b) the embryo grows into human personhood through developing complexity. Some of those taking the latter view see the embryo at less than fourteen days as entitled to ethical respect, but not yet fully a human being.

(b) Preimplantation genetic diagnosis (PGD)

62. Embryos formed in vitro (that is to say, generated in the laboratory) are selected for implantation into the womb on the basis of certain criteria. The ethical permissibility of this procedure clearly depends critically upon the status of the early embryo. Christians take three different positions on this issue:

i) PGD is an acceptable procedure if used to eliminate embryos that carry the risk of life-threatening disease, either of early on-set or, perhaps, also development later in life;

ii) selection is an ethically unacceptable form of commodification of the embryo and hence of all human life;

iii) more generally, in vitro fertilisation (IVF) procedures that involve embryo destruction through non-implantation are unacceptable.

63. In relation to option i), there is concern that its exercise might lead to unacceptable devaluation of those who are born with the relevant condition.

(c) Stem cells

64. Human embryonic stem cells, which are capable of developing into any kind of tissue, can only be obtained by the destruction of the embryo. For those who see the early embryo as a human being, this procedure is ethically unacceptable. They advocate an alternative path for stem cell research. Stem cells can be obtained from adult cells or from stored umbilical cord blood, but currently it is not known how to induce their development into all possible kinds of tissue. When this can be done, it might lead to treatments for severe degenerative diseases, such as Parkinson's Disease. Such tissue would be compatible with the person from whom the stem cells originated and there would, therefore, be no tissue rejection problems due to the introduction of genetically foreign cells. Such a procedure, if successful, does not seem to raise the same ethical difficulties as using embryonic stem cells.

(d) Therapeutic cloning

65. A different approach to problems of tissue compatibility would be to use the techniques that have led to the birth of cloned animals, in order to produce human embryos that were clones of the intended recipient's tissue. Harvesting stem cells would result in the death of the embryo at the age of about five days. The acceptability of this practice clearly depends on the ethical view taken of the early embryo. If it is already fully human, this should not be done. If it is not yet fully human, there seems the possibility of using the embryo for serious purposes not achievable through a non-embryonic route.

(e) Reproductive cloning

66. This can be clearly distinguished from therapeutic cloning since it involves the implantation of a cloned embryo with the intention of bringing a human clone to birth. Animal experiments show reproductive cloning to be grossly unsafe, with the ethically unacceptable

prevalence of wastage and malformation. Even if these problems could be overcome, there remains the ethical objection that the determining of another person's entire genetic make-up is an unacceptable use of manipulative power, an act of instrumentalisation that is contrary to human dignity.

(f) Implications for women in particular

67. The development and use of these new technologies have particular significance for women. The natural habitat of the embryo is a woman's body. Many of the procedures we consider here involve the utilisation of human egg cells, which cannot be extracted from the ovaries without invasive and painful medical intervention. The same concerns and dangers of the commodification of the embryo also apply to the women who would provide the many egg cells needed for therapeutic cloning.

2. *Developments in artificial intelligence research:*
   implications and limitations

68. At various times throughout history, the latest technology has been used to explain the workings of the human mind. The mechanical clock and the telephone exchange were once used as metaphors for the human reasoning process. Today the computer, a programmable general-purpose machine, plays this role. Following the computer metaphor, the brain is said to be a machine made of meat: human consciousness is said to be nothing more than the activity of our nerve cells. It is said that we are "programmed" to do this or that and that when we learn something, we are "programming" our brains.

69. The currency of these metaphors, together with the recent progress in AI research, raises concerns that:

(1) Humans will be as nothing more than information-processing machines and thereby lose the respect and dignity due to human persons;

(2) Human skills will be replaced by programmable learning machines;

(3) Automated decision-making technology will put sensitive human situations beyond effective human control;

(4) The sheer complexity of computer controlled systems can obscure the accountability of safety-critical systems; and

(5) Ethically responsible decisions will be delegated to computer-controlled systems.

70. While metaphors of human beings as nothing more than information processing machines may be useful in a limited technical sense, they do not address the richness of the human condition and experience as manifest through specific cultural and social contexts. The human person is based on a network of relationships constituted through provisional, embodied, contingent, meaning-producing interactions with significant others. The human relationship with the Other who is God also has these characteristics.

71. The vision of AI widely articulated through popular science fiction narratives ends either with idolatry (that ultimately we are obliged to serve the machines we have created) or hubris (that we find false salvation through our own heroic achievements). God's salvation is an embodied event of human solidarity that is a counter witness. Still, the potential for sin is found within the bounded and contingent condition of being human.

II. A Theological Response

A. LAMENT AMID SUFFERING

72. To pass in review a range of the afflictions, situations and questions which challenge our human condition – as these last pages have done – is to raise deep and troubling feelings. In response to these feelings, faith engages the heart and soul as well as the mind. Lament is one ancient response to human suffering and challenges to being human. What is lament? Lament is a form of mourning. It is also more. It is more purposeful and more instinctive than mourning. Lamenting is both an individual and a communal act which signals that relationships have gone awry. While lamenting is about past events, it also has present and future dimensions. It acknowledges the brokenness of the present because of injustice. It instinctively creates a link between healing and mourning, a link which makes new, just relationships possible in future. Lament is generous and not grudging,

explicit not generalised, unafraid to contain petitions and confident that they will be heard. Lament is not utilitarian: It is as primal as the child's need to cry.

73. The cry of lament, while ostensibly wrought from the human heart in certain situations, is filled with enigmatic energies, unbearable urges, moments both profane and sacred. Lament is more than railing against suffering, breast-beating or a confession of guilt. It is a coil of suffering and hope, of awareness and memory, anger and relief, desires for vengeance, forgiveness and healing. It is our way of bearing the unbearable, both individually and communally. It is a wailing of the human soul, a barrage of tears, reproaches, petitions, praise and hopes which beat against the heart of God. It is supremely and truly human: "Jesus wept" (John 11:35) as he beheld the reality of suffering and death.

74. How do we as Christians respond to these challenges? Where do we begin? A first step is to try to reach a common theological understanding of what it means to be a human being.

B. CREATED IN THE IMAGE OF GOD

1. *Jesus Christ as the image of God*

75. In faith Christians look to a human face and in that face they see the image and glory of the invisible God (Mark 9:2.8; Col. 1:15). This is no ordinary seeing. We know that the face of the Galilean is not literally the face of God; faith is not the same as literal "sight" and may indeed be better compared to the action of a sightless person reaching out to touch and feel the contour of a face they cannot "see".

> *Affirmation:* **Jesus Christ through his life, death and resurrection is victorious over sin and death, restores true humanity, empowers life, and brings hope for the end of inhumanity, injustice and suffering.**

76. The human face in which that glory is shown to us is the face of one person: Jesus Christ. But what we see and know of him informs and shapes our awareness of the identity, the worth and the calling of every person (2 Cor. 5:16-17). More than that, Jesus Christ insists that he is with us, that wherever we may be looking from he stands among us, in our place. So what we learn as we keep our attention focused on Jesus (Heb. 12:2) is not abstract information about a foreign kind of human life. Rather our understanding and enactment of what it is to be human develops in a living dialogue between the voices of our own society, its needs, its insights, its aspirations, and the word which is spoken to us, addressing those very needs, insights and aspirations — to challenge as well as to affirm.

2. The mystery of human being

77. The mystery of the true human being we see in Jesus, the Word made flesh, is unsearchable. Our attempts to investigate and understand human nature cannot exhaust the worth, the depth and the dignity which belong to each person as created and loved by God. As we acknowledge, with faith and awe, the holy mystery of God, we see and reverence that same mystery in the person of Jesus and we must also see and reverence a reflection of that same mystery in every person.

3. The image of true humanity is not alien to any community

78. There can be no single, definitive picture or icon of Christ. There is a definitive record of Jesus; it is given in Scripture and received by people in every time and place through the living Tradition of faith. From all this, we can discern the indelible character of Jesus' life and ministry, death and resurrection. He remains "the same yesterday, today, for ever" (Heb. 13:8) and "his words will not pass away" (Mark 13:31 and parallels). Yet the Spirit which enables us to see the face of Christ as the true image of God and of our humanity is for ever new. The Spirit teaches us all things and reminds us of all that Christ has said whilst leading us to hear Christ's words anew at every stage in the life of each person, in the life of the Christian community and in human history. By the gift of the Spirit, Christ's word is proclaimed in the languages of many nations (Acts 2:8), so that all may recognise him as bearing our likeness as well as God's.

4. *Christian understanding and the struggles and insights of the wider world*

79. Christian understanding of what it is to be human unfolds through shared engagement and meditation in the community of faith. That community is not isolated from or unaffected by the world. Believers share the political and social struggles of troubled and threatened groups and peoples. Just as importantly, believers share the exploration of human identity undertaken in the communities of science and the arts. A fuller theological account of who and what we are as humans emerges from the Church's prayerful engagement with each of these realms, as we keep the person of Jesus in focus.

5. *The image of true humanity is not known in the abstract*

80. The focus of faith on Jesus as the point of reference for understanding what it is to be human has a decisive consequence. It means that this understanding can never be a matter of detached thinking. As Jesus was to be found in company with people pushed aside in their own society, so our understanding of all humanity must be informed by our engagement with those whom society marginalises. Just as Jesus was no casual observer of his suffering sisters and brothers but was with them to serve and to transform, so that all could have life in its fullness (Mark 10:45; Luke 4:18; John 10:10), so we cannot assert a merely theoretical or passive understanding of human nature. For Christians to be passive in the face of suffering and injustice would make nonsense of any claim to "understand". As noted in the discussion on the method of the study, and elsewhere, this is the fundamental awareness that has informed this project.

6. *Persons and relationship*

81. Jesus is revealed as the one who gives himself away (Phil. 2:5-11). This self-giving manifests his relationship with the Father and the Holy Spirit – the one who sent him and the one whom he sends (John 14:24; 16:7.8). So it dawned upon the early Church that, in the light of Jesus, God must be worshipped and apprehended by faith as Triune, as three "persons" in one "nature", where, by the power and mystery of eternal love, Father, Son and Spirit live in perfect mutuality and unity. So it becomes clear to those who reflect on the face of Jesus that true personhood cannot be understood individualistically, but only as we look at human persons in relationship.

Affirmation: **The presence of the image of God in each human person and in the whole of humanity affirms the essentially relational character of human nature and emphasises human dignity, potentiality and creativity, as well as human creatureliness, finitude and vulnerability.**

7. *The image of God as relational*

82. In the light of its trinitarian perspective the Church has found special significance in the account of human creation in Genesis. In Genesis 1:26 God says that human beings are to be made not with reference only to themselves, not according to their kind (like other creatures), but "in our image, in our likeness". Human beings are not like their own kind, but are to be like God. Here it is clear that being made in God's image is foundational for all human beings, male and female (Gen. 1:26-27). Approaching the text with a trinitarian understanding, it is also clear that this image, in which all humanity is created, is first and foremost relational. As we draw together the text of Genesis 1 and the figure of Christ Jesus, we perceive that we truly image God only in communion with Christ and with one another. In communion with Christ we are drawn by the Holy Spirit into relationship with the Father, becoming capable of working together (synergia) with the Triune God for the fulfilment of God's loving design for the whole creation. This insight into the essentially relational character of true human identity before God has become a major key to addressing contemporary challenges to humanity in the light of Christian faith. As the current Faith and Order study on Ethnic Identity, National Identity and the Search for the Unity of the Church puts it, "[h]uman beings are made in, by and for a community, a human characteristic which finds its expression in many forms and under many names". (ETHNAT study document, FO/2004:27, Faverges Report, §12.)

8. *The dignity of each person*

83. The importance of the individual is not negated by emphasising the central place of relationship in interpreting the human condition. Some social ideals have tended towards treating the individual person

as a means to an end, or as significant only by virtue of her or his contribution to the group. But the image of God, while it can never be fulfilled in an individual who chooses to be closed off from God or from the other, can never be effaced from any person. In many circumstances the Church will rightly defend the cause or dignity of one person against the antagonism or prejudice of a whole society, recognising that the least or most isolated individual is infinitely precious in the sight of God.

9. True humanity and false human "ideals"

84. Seeing the face of Jesus (and the harsh reality of his life as the incarnate God) we are also compelled to confront and question many alluring images of the human ideal. As noted in the earlier discussion on disability, in contemporary cultures there is often a pervasive assumption that only a "perfect" person can reflect true humanity, where the "perfect" image is assumed to be successful, young, attractive and not disabled. But in Jesus we see true humanity (the image of God) not only at the point when his appearance reflects visible glory, on the mount of Transfiguration. We also see the same true humanity just as clearly when his face and body are deformed by suffering. Re-reading the text of Isaiah 53, Christians have identified Jesus with the one who "had no form or majesty that we should look at him, and no beauty that we should desire him" (Isa. 53:2) and so have been powerfully reminded that equal human dignity and worth are given to every human being, the physically disabled along with outstanding athletes, women able to bear children along with those who cannot, persons who struggle to survive as much as those who prosper.

10. The divine image gives value to all human lives

85. Christians look through this Christ-centred lens in seeking true understanding of human identity, worth and purpose. This does not mean that they ignore or discredit secular wisdom. But they are compelled to resist all attempts to draw distinctions between human beings, and the degree of value or importance that should be ascribed to them. At many times and in many places, pharaohs, kings and rulers are said to be "the image of God", but in the text of Genesis and in the Christian Tradition all human beings are made in the image of

God: male and females rich and poor, Jew and Gentile, old and young, slave and free. The claim which faith makes on behalf of every person is not that she or he be valued according to a measure of aptitudes, abilities or achievements, but that she or he be valued as made by God to be loved and to love, and as sharing in the divine image which is gifted to – not earned or discovered by – all human beings.

11. Human life as growing in the image

86. When St Paul writes of Christians as reflecting God's glory in the face of Jesus, he writes in terms of transformation ("from one degree of glory to another", 2 Cor. 3:18). So we are led to recognise that human beings are called to grow into the image of Christ, who is himself the true and complete image of God. This awareness has long been expressed in the theology of the eastern churches by marking a distinction between the image and the likeness of God: "All human beings are made in God's image; to be in his likeness belongs only to those who through much love have subjected their freedom to God" (Diadochos of Photike, 5th century). Western traditions have not usually made the same distinction, but have equally recognised the dimension of calling and growth that belongs to true personhood.

12. Human embodiment

87. If the Christian understanding of true humanity is rooted in reflection on the person of Jesus Christ it will neither denigrate nor idolise the human body. The love of God was fully embodied in Jesus. The truth of the incarnation and the nature of the gospels underline the fact that the paradigm of true holiness and humanity is one who shared bodily pain and joy and who, in his work of healing, treated with seriousness and compassion the bodily needs of others.

13. Theology and experience

88. By careful reflection we can arrive at a statement of what it is to be human, as seen in the light of Jesus. This statement is important, particularly when it binds the churches together in common faith and witness. However, the mothers and grandmothers who return each week to the Plaza de Mayo in Buenos Aires to hold up the pictures of the disappeared whom they refuse to forget; those who struggle to

feed their own children or to defend them from the depredations of HIV/AIDS; those who exhaust themselves in the support of their neighbour in need: all these may have grasped and lived such an understanding, for they live very close to the face of Christ.

C. THE PLACE OF HUMANITY WITHIN CREATION AS A WHOLE

1. *Relationship with that which is other than ourselves*

89. In the previous section we have been reflecting on the person of Jesus as the focus for Christian understanding of human persons made in God's image. Central to these reflections is the relational character of true human life. This relatedness or partnership with God and one another for which we are made corresponds to the gift of differentiation, or diversity. When Jesus befriended and ate with people of all sorts, people seldom seen together, he showed how the gift of relatedness overcomes fear of difference to create true community, true koinonia. Similarly this statement, and the whole of our study, has developed through engagement and friendship within many different cultures and communities.

> *Affirmation:* **Human beings are created to be in relationship not only with God and each other but with the whole of creation, respecting and being responsible for all living creatures and the whole created order.**

2. *The relationship of humans to the rest of creation*

90. One of the ways in which we see that humans are created in the image of God is the way in which we have been entrusted with the privilege of sharing with God the responsibility of taking care of the whole creation. God created us to be in loving relationship not only with one another, but also with the entire creation. God's own love and care sustain everything that exists, clothing the grass of the field (Luke 12:28) and being aware even of the fall of a sparrow (Mt. 10:29). And it is God's intent that the whole creation, everything in

heaven and earth, should share in the ultimate liberation and unity which will be set forth in Christ, through whom all things came into being (Eph. 1:10; John 1:3). Meanwhile, we are called to relationship of loving care with the wider creation, acknowledging and taking responsibility for our place within the dynamic interconnected and interdependent whole of creation. The fact that God created all things good means that this co-responsibility, however exacting it may be, will always occasion delight and celebration.

91. Another feature of being in the image of God is that humans are made to be "co-creators" with God (Gen. 2:19). Because we are not God, our creativity is limited by our creatureliness. Nevertheless we have the God-given capacity to explore, envisage and bring into being new possibilities within the created order. It is not apart from, but in union with the whole created order that we are called to praise the creator (Ps. 148) and to co-operate with God as active partners in developing and maintaining the health of creation.

D. SIN AND THE IMAGE OF GOD

1. The nature of sin is made clear by reflection on God's image

> *Affirmation:* **Sin is a reality which cannot be ignored nor minimised, for it results both in the alienation of humanity from God and in the brokenness of the world, its communities, and the individuals which make up those communities.**

92. For Christian disciples, Jesus represents all they are created to be and called to become. In him we can grasp what God intends for humankind. Such an image of what it means to be a human being dignifies our flesh and frailty, subverts our notions of power and rule and challenges us to interpret the signs which our world manifests in a new way. But when we look to or listen to Jesus, we are struck, too, by our own failure to be what God intends. The light of Christ offers a beacon to all who share his humanity; it also sheds light on the sin of all who share his humanity.

93. When we speak of humankind made in God's image, we inevitably have to speak also of the spoiling of that image. And just as the reflection of Christ and of God's being in our humanity is bound up with our relatedness to God and to one another, so it is with our sin. Relationships which in Christ are characterised by love, truthfulness and reverence are replaced by aggression, exploitation, deceit, brokenness and violence.

2.   The radical nature of sin

94. The sin of human beings contributes to, and belongs within, a wider context: the disorder and evil which affect the whole of creation. Paul expresses this graphically when he writes of the "whole creation groaning" (Rom. 8:22). Sometimes the very word "sin" seems too lame or moralistic to describe the depth and power of all that assaults and harms God's good creation, or the sheer destructiveness and wickedness which human beings manifest. Nonetheless, Christian faith forbids us ever to suppose that even the most obscene enemies of human wellbeing are not themselves made in the image of God: they remain human persons, neither to be exonerated from personal responsibility nor to be denied justice and humanity.

3.   Sin in the context of hope

95. Realistic observation of the harm we human beings do to each other and to the creatures around us, and to the very earth itself, leads us to conclude that our human condition is radically warped, that the image is distorted. The aspects of human brokenness, conflict and perplexity that have been touched on in Part I lead many – both those who suffer and those who observe their plight – to lose hope. But the Christian consciousness of sin and evil comes not so much from human introspection or brutal observation as from seeing the wounded love of Christ and hearing the forgiving and challenging word of Christ.

96. Those who see their own sin in the light of God's countenance are led not to despair or cynicism but to repentance in hope. The Holy Spirit gives a dynamic of hope to the understanding of human sin, a dynamic illustrated in the gospels as the encounter with Jesus leads to repentance, repentance leads to renewal, and renewal leads to the call-

ing and empowerment to act with Jesus in the world. This dynamic is misunderstood both by those who rest on the assurance that God will forgive "anyway", whatever we do (forgetting that God calls us to repentance), and by those who envisage a god preoccupied with judgement and punishment (forgetting that God calls us to repentance *in order that we may live*).

> *Affirmation:* **True humanity is most clearly seen in self-emptying (kenotic) love, the love expressed most profoundly in the person of Jesus of Nazareth: human beings are created to love and to be loved as Jesus loved.**

E. THE NEW CREATION IN CHRIST

1. New life offered to the world in Christ

97. The New Testament tells of Jesus Christ not just as the expression or image of God's nature, but as the very embodiment, the incarnation of God: divine Word and Love in flesh. In Phil. 2:5-11 this embodiment is set within a pathway of profound self-emptying which leads to the cross. All Christians trace the source of the possibility of new life to Jesus Christ, his life, his death and his resurrection. All give glory to God for the depths of Christ's identification with us, knowing that our hope was born out of this costly identification, this radical embracing of our condition.

2. Interpretations of Christ's reconciling work

98. Differing strands of Christian tradition have emphasised various themes or focal points within the whole, manifold witness of the New Testament. Many, for example, have given foremost place to the preaching of the cross, as showing the limitless engagement of God's love with the most intractable depths of the human condition. Here the cross is preached as the point at which the record of human debt was cancelled by God, the powers of evil disarmed and new life made available to us (Col. 2:13-15). Other traditions emphasise the place of the cross within the context of the incarnation and ascension – the

divine Word taking our flesh and raising our human life to the right hand of God, giving us "power to become children of God" (John 1:12). Others again have emphasised the centrality of the life, work and teaching of Christ and affirmed the transformative power of this life (with the death and resurrection which are inextricably bound up with it). These differing emphases have found expression in deeply influential patterns of spiritual, ethical and devotional life. They have also given distinctive colours to the interpretation of Christian anthropology. Christians need to grow in awareness, both of each others' perspectives and of their impact upon theoretical and practical responses to the human condition.

99. The resurrection and ascension of Christ signal the vindication of his being and life as "the faithful witness" (Rev. 1:5) and the triumph of his love over all that afflicts and distorts creation. Yet even the risen and ascended one still bears the wounds of crucifixion. The raised yet wounded body tells us that the risen one is no other than the one who made himself nothing, it expresses Christ's continuing identification with and intercession for the wounded on earth, and reminds Christ's followers that when they are weak they are strong (2 Cor. 12:10).

3. The human appropriation of new life

100. Our involvement in the new life offered to us through Christ's death and resurrection is shown in the New Testament at once as a matter purely of grace and faith, and as involving our total embodied selves and community. As sheer gift, there is no requirement for us to "pay" for the new humanity – which is the very life of free gracious relationship. It is God's gift to us in Christ.

101. We receive this gift in the act of faith, "believing in the heart and confessing with the lips" (cf. Rom. 10:9) the supremacy of the risen Jesus. Yet, responding to the offer of the whole Christ – active, suffering, crucified, risen – involves us in a new, social embodiment, in Christ the new Adam, as members together of the one body of Christ, sharing the one Spirit (Eph. 2:15-16, 4:4), living stones built together into a holy and spirit-filled temple (1 Peter 2:4-5). So the new minting of the image of God involves a new communion: koinonia.

This koinonia – a relatedness to God and to one another – is an essential characteristic of the Church, as expressed in many ecumenical documents (see, for example, *The Nature and Purpose of the Church*, Faith and Order Paper No. 181, §§48-60, and "The Nature and Mission of the Church", FO/2004:32, §§25-35).

102. The Spirit of God, which according to the creation narratives was moving over the face of the waters in the beginning (Gen. 1:2), is also at the origin of the new creation. At the day of Pentecost, all those present in Jerusalem are united in one proclamation and doxology (Acts 2). The barriers of language and pride, that were at Babel at the roots of confusion and dispersion, have been overcome. By the reception of the Spirit of God who raised Jesus from the dead, the disciples are born to a new personal life and a new community (Rom. 8:11). All are baptised into one body and are made to drink of one Spirit. Henceforth there is no longer Jew or Greek, slave or free, male or female, for all are one in Christ. Nevertheless the varieties of gifts, services and activities are not only legitimate but necessary for the building up of the body of Christ, the service of the Good News and the glory of God (1 Cor. 12:4-7, 12-23; Gal. 3:28). The uniqueness and richness of the individual persons are thus infinitely valued together with the necessity and complementarity of their communal dimensions.

4. Baptism and new humanity in Christ

103. Baptism is the sacramental sign given to the Christian community to express and embody the totality of new life in Christ. It is the birth-place of the new humanity because in it we are identified indelibly with Christ crucified and risen. In baptism the personal freedom and dignity of each candidate is expressed and transformed through the confession of faith and commitment and the prayer of the faithful. The water of baptism signifies both cleansing from sin and the divine source of new life. Those who pass through the water of baptism are brought into a community of profound equality within which divisive difference is banished, while diversity of gift and calling is honoured. Through baptism, and the acts of anointing, confirmation or other forms of admission to church membership that may be associated with it, Christians are also called to make Christ known and to

serve God's reign by living and acting for the relief of need, the righting of injustice and the advancing of peace and mutuality in creation. The consequence of sharing, through baptism, in the death and resurrection of Jesus is that, as Paul emphasised, "we might walk in newness of life" (Rom. 6:4).

104. Since the rite of baptism is held in common by so many churches, it is also a constant challenge to the divisions which mar our witness to Christ as the prince of peace and the one in whom all nations are called to meet. As put succinctly by the section on baptism in the convergence document *Baptism, Eucharist and Ministry* (BEM): "The need to recover baptismal unity is at the heart of the ecumenical task, as it is central to the realisation of genuine partnership within the Christian communities". (§6, commentary). The mutual recognition of baptism among the churches is fundamental to the churches' search for unity, as the current Faith and Order Study on Baptism emphasises, and it constitutes "a basis for their increasing common witness, worship and service" ("One Baptism: Towards Mutual Recognition of Christian Initiation", FO/2004:30, §74).

> *Affirmation:* **Christians, baptised into the body of Christ and enlivened by the Holy Spirit, are called to be the new humanity, to grow into the likeness of God and, together, to carry on the work of Christ in the world. As the Church, Christians are the sign to the world of unity with God and with each other.**

105. When Christ was baptised in the River Jordan, a voice was heard from heaven declaring his identity as Son of God. For the newly baptised Christian, baptism marks his or her being clothed with the new humanity which comes from Jesus (1 Cor. 12:12-13; Gal. 3:27; Col. 3:9-10). And just as the Spirit descended upon Jesus and anointed him at his baptism, so everyone baptised in Christ is anointed and sent to bring the good news to the poor and let the oppressed go free (Luke 3:21-22; 4:18).

Every person who receives and responds to this anointing and commissioning is then involved throughout life in a Spirit-led striving to "become what we are" – as a member of the new creation in Christ.

106. The expression "baptismal life" may, as the study document "One Baptism…" indicates, properly be applied to the whole process of pre-baptismal formation, baptism itself and post-baptismal "continuing formation into Christ" (§6).

5. The eucharist

107. In the Eucharist the community of the baptised takes bread and wine and in offering these gifts is reminded of its daily dependence on God's kindness to us in the material creation and of the care and thankfulness with which all are called to cultivate and share these goods. Through the epiclesis of the Holy Spirit the bread and wine are sanctified to become for us the body and blood of Christ and a foretaste of the new creation. As we take, bless, break and share these gifts in remembrance of Christ's death and resurrection, we are taken into the pattern of Christ's self-giving in love and are renewed in the kenotic dynamic of God's image in him. In the epiclesis the Holy Spirit is also invoked on the gathering of the faithful, so that they may be sanctified and receive the communion of the Holy Spirit and the fullness of the Kingdom of heaven.

108. In some traditions this dynamic is expressed in the symbolic act of foot-washing. When Christians within the church wash one another's feet, they are not only given a vivid reminder of the action of Jesus recorded in John 13. They also find themselves powerfully drawn into the self-giving service which this action expressed.

109. So, as we receive Christ's body in the Eucharist we recognise ourselves as Christ's body, and are challenged by the awareness of his brokenness. "Some aspects of God's image in Christ can only be reflected in the Church as the body of Christ by the full inclusion and honouring of those who have bodies that are likewise impaired" ("A Church of All and for All – An Interim Statement", Ecumenical Disabilities Advocates Network [EDAN], §29).

110. The table-fellowship of the Holy Communion or koinonia is to be seen as linked with the inclusive practice of Jesus in eating with outcasts and "bad characters" within the society of his time. So we are bound to share Christ's endeavour to overcome ancient hostilities and barriers to fellowship (Eph. 2:11-22), to welcome the stranger and

alien, and to create inclusive communities which afford space to people of diverse needs, cultures and aspirations.

111. In their eucharistic practice the churches struggle with the question of ecumenical hospitality and openness. But all share the vision of an all-embracing community, inspired by the practice and teaching of Jesus of Nazareth and pointing to the ultimate unity of humankind. This shared vision challenges all the churches to submit their own culture and practice to serious and self-critical scrutiny. If churches fail to welcome others as God in Christ has welcomed us, and to reflect this appropriately at the centre of church life and worship, they are failing the crying need of a divided world.

6. Christian anthropology and hope

112. The promise of God's glory is also re-awakened in the Eucharist as we are given a foretaste of the heavenly banquet prepared for all humankind and have our feet directed towards the new heaven and new earth which awaits us:

> Remembering therefore this our Saviour's command and all that has been done for us: the cross, the tomb, the resurrection on the third day, the ascension into heaven, the sitting at the right hand, the second and glorious coming again…we praise you, we bless you, we give thanks to you, O Lord, and we pray to you, our God (*Liturgy of John Chrysostom*, Oxford University Press, 1995).

In this way the Eucharist focuses the whole thrust and direction of Christian anthropology, which is oriented by hope for that which is already achieved by Christ, yet still to come.

113. Since this hope arises from Jesus Christ, who took the form of a servant or slave and humbled himself even to death, Christ therefore gives rise to hope even where there is nothing to hope for. In company with Jesus are those patriarchs and prophets, saints and martyrs whose lives bear witness to that hope against hope which springs from obedience to God who "brings to life things that are not". This wide "communion of saints" forms a context of hope and encouragement for all those whose human flourishing is challenged by violence, need, impairment and injustice, and for those who grow weary

in the service and care of others (Heb. 12:1). It points to heaven not as a dream or distraction from endeavour on earth, but as the assurance of the final vindication of God's children and the knowledge that in the Lord their labour is not in vain.

114. The hope which springs from Christ also encourages us to let go of our terror of failure, decline and death. In the light of the promise of new, risen life we are strengthened to accept human limitation as wisdom directs us, and to entrust to God and to our neighbour the tasks we cannot fulfil.

> *Affirmation:* **Humanity finds its ultimate fulfilment, together with the whole created order, when God brings all things to perfection in Christ.**

115. "It does not yet appear what we shall be, but we know that when he [Christ] appears we shall be like him, because we shall see him as he is" (1 John 3:2). The final hope for the Christian community and believer is expressed in varying ways by different strands and theologies within the Christian Tradition: as theosis ("deification"), or being raised into the divine life (Irenaeus), as "finding our rest in God" (Augustine). But for each, this represents the fulfilment of all for which humanity was formed within creation. Through the judgement and generosity of God in Christ the meek of the earth will be seen as bearing God's glory (Irenaeus). This promise and hope is inescapably communal: no one is raised in isolation from the neighbour! It is a promise and hope for "all nations" and for "a new heaven and earth" (Rev. 21) – for the totality of what God has made and loves. And because it is a promise and hope founded in Jesus Christ, who knew with compassion what was in a person, it will mean not the obliteration but the exaltation of all that contributes to the blessed diversity of our earthly, embodied humanity.

III. A Call to the Churches

116. Part I of this text has traced several of the new challenges posed today to the understanding of the human person created in the image of God. Part II has developed ecumenical theological reflections on the meaning and destiny of the human person created in the image of God, an image fully revealed through the life, death and resurrection of Jesus Christ. Part III now draws the consequences from these reflections, encouraging the churches to work together, in light of their common faith, to address such challenges facing humanity today.

A. A Basis for Common Confession, Reflection, Witness and Service

1. *Common understandings*

117. The churches have an ample shared basis for witness and work in the face of all that challenges human flourishing. Common understandings of the mystery of the human person, created in the image of God, destined to live in community within the wider creation, constitute a large and solid basis for ecumenical confession, reflection, witness and service. Our churches agree, for example, on the unique worth and dignity of every human being, called to live and find fulfilment in the human community and to experience and preserve harmony with all of creation. They agree that despite the vast variety of cultures and contexts, all human beings share a common human identity and predicament. And the churches agree that the full richness of this mystery is revealed and offered in the person of Jesus Christ, the perfect image of God, who, through his life, his self-giving death and glorious resurrection, has overcome the forces of sin, evil and death at work in human persons, human communities and creation.

118. The revelation in Christ of what it means to live in the image of God invites Christians to work with believers of other faiths, as well as with non-believers, in affirming human dignity and opposing all the forces which threaten and cheapen life today. Recognising in every person an equal, irreplaceable dignity, all religions and convictions must guard against the trap of sectarianism and exclusion. Churches will be able to collaborate effectively only if they first listen respectfully to each other.

119. Ecumenical theological reflection gives support and encouragement to the churches' common witness on what it means to be human made in the image of God. The churches are called to offer their witness and diaconal service in response to such challenges to humanity as brokenness (violence, poverty and HIV/AIDS), disabilities, and new technologies (genetic manipulation and artificial intelligence research). In each case the churches' common convictions about the nature of the human person made in the image of God offer the basis for their reflection and action together. Some examples: because each person, being made in God's image, is of infinite worth the churches work together to end violence, whether in the home or between nations. They witness together to the need for just distribution of resources. They work to enable disabled persons to participate fully in the life of the Church and the wider society. They refuse to accept genetic research which treats life as a commodity, and human beings as objects. Where Christians and churches differ on the best approach to particular issues (as seen in the discussion of developments in genetics, §§61-62 above), this need not deny their common understanding of the human person, nor impede their common witness.

2. Legitimate – and other – diversity

120. As churches seek to reflect and work together they may discover certain differences in the theological approach or terminology used. For instance, from Gen. 1:26 the distinction is made by some between "image" and "likeness", and the call is made for persons to grow from the "image" into the "likeness" of God. The concept of theosis, expressing the goal of this growth, is then the natural result of humanity's being created in the image of God. Others, however, fear that this notion may blur the distinction between God and human beings. Again there are differing interpretations of how sin impacts the image of God in human beings: is the image obliterated and lost, or marred and distorted?

121. Other differences have to do with how Christians and the churches can best respond to challenges to the worth and dignity of human beings. Churches which own a common basic understanding of the human person, and share a commitment to witness to God's will for healing and wholeness in the world God has made, may dis-

agree on the strategies to be followed, and the concrete choices to be made, in addressing particular issues. This became clear in the course of this study through the analysis of contemporary challenges to the human person and community.

122. There are, of course, issues of understanding and practice in which Christians and churches differ seriously, even fundamentally – issues where it is a matter not of legitimate diversity but of division. Moreover, such differences occur not only between and among churches, but also within particular churches. Many of the most divisive issues among and within churches today are related to human sexuality. Human sexuality is intrinsic to being human. However, too often it becomes a source of human suffering (illustrated by stories of sex workers and persons with HIV/AIDS above), as well as a cause of church division. Churches today are challenged to engage in frank and serious theological discussion that begins with an affirmation of human sexuality as a gift of God and a joyous expression of life and love. Reflecting on biblical teachings, churches in this discussion are called to address divergent convictions about human sexuality in its various forms in a spirit of humility and mutual respect.

123. Most differences in understanding and strategy in the realm of theological anthropology need not prevent our churches from facing together the challenges to humanity today. In many areas of need, the churches can exercise a common (and therefore far more effective) witness to the world in defence of human beings made in the image of God.

B. FACING CHALLENGES TOGETHER

124. In order to respond more faithfully to their calling, to fulfil their responsibility more adequately and to be an authentic sign and instrument of reconciliation in the world, the churches must continue their efforts to overcome their divisions, to speak with one voice and to co-ordinate their action. In this effort unity, witness and service are inseparable: growth in witness and service brings growth in unity, and growth in unity brings growth in witness and service.

125. Common reflection, witness and action on behalf of the human person made in the image of God is not optional, but is intrinsic to our faith and to the church's calling. In working together the churches need to mobilize all their theological resources, beginning from common baptism. Our baptism unites us to Christ, and therefore to one another. This forms the basis for koinonia which, even if it cannot yet fully be expressed in a common Eucharist, nevertheless calls all in the body of Christ to common witness and service in the world. In baptism, the relationship between God and humanity that had been broken by sin is restored, old barriers are broken down, and a new community is created in which human dignity and worth are recognised, and relationships of love are restored. "...baptism...has ethical implications which not only call for personal sanctification, but also motivate Christians to strive for the realization of the will of God in all realms of life" (BEM, "Baptism", §10).

126. The common understanding of humanity made in the image of God which the churches share gives them the ability – if not always the courage or will – to identify, clarify and face together even the most serious issues which divide them. In facing them together our churches may hope to grow in mutual understanding and trust. They may hope to overcome their divisions, or at least to reduce their impact upon the lives of the churches concerned. This is all the more imperative since divisions within and among churches often reflect differences in the surrounding culture, so that reconciliation within and among churches is often a contribution to healing in the wider society.

C. Ten Common Affirmations

127. This Faith and Order study has led to the following Ten Common Affirmations on Theological Anthropology. These are offered as a basis for the churches' common reflection and action on the challenges facing humanity today:

1. All human beings are created in the image of God and Jesus Christ is the one in whom true humanity is perfectly realized.

2. The presence of the image of God in each human person and in the whole of humanity affirms the essentially relational character of human nature and emphasises human dignity, potentiality and creativity, as well as human creatureliness, finitude and vulnerability.

3. True humanity is most clearly seen in self-emptying (kenotic) love, the love expressed most profoundly in the person of Jesus of Nazareth: human beings are created to love and to be loved as Jesus loved.

4. Human beings are created to be in relationship not only with God and each other but with the whole of creation, respecting and being responsible for all living creatures and the whole created order.

5. All human beings, though created in the image of God, are inevitably affected by individual and corporate sin.

6. Sin is a reality which cannot be ignored nor minimised, for it results both in the alienation of humanity from God and in the brokenness of the world, its communities, and the individuals which make up those communities.

7. Sin can pervert or distort, but cannot finally destroy, what it means to be human.

8. Jesus Christ through his life, death and resurrection is victorious over sin and death, restores true humanity, empowers life, and brings hope for the end of inhumanity, injustice and suffering.

9. Christians, baptised into the Body of Christ and enlivened by the Holy Spirit, are called to be the new humanity, to grow into the likeness of God and, together, to carry on the work of Christ in the world. As the Church, Christians are the sign to the world of unity with God and with each other.

10. Humanity finds its ultimate fulfilment, together with the whole created order, when God brings all things to perfection in Christ.

D. INVITATION TO THE CHURCHES

128. On the basis of the Ten Affirmations given above, the churches are invited:

- to affirm the image of God in every person;
- to be gracious and inclusive communities where persons are accepted as created in the image of God, welcomed as sisters and brothers in Christ, and challenged to grow, in the power of the Holy Spirit, more fully into the divine likeness;
- to work for the visible unity of the Church with penitence and vigour, knowing that the divisions between Christians often reflect and exacerbate the brokenness of the human community.

129. The churches are also encouraged to continue reflection on the implications of our belief that human beings are created in the image of God, by considering among others the following questions:

- How can we cultivate the human creative capacity to act justly and to be merciful?
- How can we protest the widening gulf between the poor and the rich and work for a just distribution of the world's resources?
- How can we care for victims of war, forced migration, famine, illiteracy, and HIV/AIDS and other diseases?
- How can we break the silence surrounding violence against women and children, and engage in ministries of healing?
- How can we engage with the scientific community in exploring and developing responsible new technologies related to the beginning and end of human life, e.g. selective reproduction, stem cell research, cloning, euthanasia?
- How can we affirm the worth and dignity of all persons irrespective of gender, sexuality, race, ethnicity, nationality, age, ability, religion, faith or no faith?
- How can we encourage one another to affirm human sexuality as both gift and responsibility, and to explore its implications for the life of the Church?

- How, taking account both of the Christian Tradition and of scientific and other contemporary insights into the nature of gender, can we explore together the theological, pastoral and ecclesial significance of gender in the life of the Church?
- How can we be makers and keepers of peace among persons, communities, churches and nations?
- How can we celebrate and create beauty in the world in which we live?

Bibliography

English

Jürgen Moltmann, Man: *Christian Anthropology in the Conflicts of the Present*, trans. by John Sturdy, London, SPCK, 1974.

Jerome Murphy-O'Connor, *Becoming Human Together: The Pastoral Anthropology of St. Paul*, Dublin, Veritas Publications; Delaware, Michael Glasier, 1982.

Kallistos Ware, *Introduction to John Climacus: The Ladder of Divine Ascent*, trans. by Colm Luibheid and Norman Russell, Classics of Western Spirituality, New York, Paulist Press, 1982, especially pp.28-34.

Christos Yannaras, *The Freedom of Morality*, trans. by Elizabeth Briere, Contemporary Greek Theologians, No. 3, Crestwood NY, St. Vladimir's Seminary Press, 1984.

Vladimir Lossky, *In the Image and Likeness of God*, New York, St Valadimir's Press, 1985.

Lars Thunberg, "The Human Person as Image of God. I. Eastern Christianity", in *Christian Spirituality: Origins to the Twelfth Century*, ed. by B. McGinn and John Meyendorff in collaboration with Jean Leclercq, New York, Crossroad, 1985, pp.291-312.

John Zizioulas, *Being as Communion: Studies in Personhood and the Church*, London, Darton, Longmann and Todd, 1985.

Panayotis Nellas, *Deification in Christ: The Nature of the Human Person*, New York, St Vladimir's Press, 1987.

Edward Schillebeeckx, *Church: The Human Story of God*, trans. by John Bowden, New York, Crossroad, 1990.

Sallie McFague, *The Body of God: An Ecological Theology*, Minneapolis, Fortress Press, 1993.

Louis-Marie Chauvet, *Symbol and Sacrament: A Sacramental Reinterpretation of Christian Existence*, Collegeville, The Liturgical Press, 1995.

Elisabeth Moltmann-Wendel, *I am My Body: A Theology of Embodiment*, trans. by John Bowden, New York, Continuum, 1995.

Mercy Amba Oduyoye, *Daughters of Anowa: African Women and Patriarchy*, Maryknoll NY, Orbis Books, 1995.

John Hull, *On Sight and Insight: A Journey into the World of Blindness*, Oxford, Oneworld, 1997.

Wolfhart Pannenberg, *Anthropology in Theological Perspective*, trans. by Matthew J. O'Connell, Edinburgh, Continuum International Publishing Group - T&T Clarke, 1999.

Ann O'Hara, *In the Embrace of God: Feminist Approaches to Theological Anthropology*, Maryknoll NY, Orbis Books, 2003.

Timothy Bradshaw, ed., *The Way Forward? Christian Voices on Homosexuality and the Church*, Grand Rapids MI, Eerdmans, 2004.

Commission on Faith and Witness of the Canadian Council of Churches, *Becoming Human: Theological Anthropology in an Age of Engineering Life, Christian Reflections for Further Discussion*, Toronto, Canadian Council of Churches, 2005.

Dwight Hopkins, *Being Human: Race, Culture, Religion*, Minneapolis, Fortress Press, 2005.

German

Neuner, P., "Ergebnisse der Hirnforschung als Herausforderungen an Theologie und Glauben. Eine Vorüberlegung zur dogmatischen Betrachtung", in: Günther Rager (Hg.), *Ich und mein Gehirn: Persönliches Erleben, verantwortliches Handeln und objektive Wissenschaft*, Freiburg (Breisgau); München, Alber 2000, pp.201-238.

Körtner, Ulrich H.J.: *Unverfügbarkeit des Lebens? Grundfragen der Bioethik.* Neukirchen-Vluyn, Neukirchener Verlag, 2001.

Andrade, Barbara: „Erbsünde" – oder Vergebung aus Gnade?,. Frankfurt/M. 2002.

Fischer, Johannes, *Medizin- und bioethische Perspektiven. Beiträge zur Urteilsbildung im Bereich von Medizin und Biologie.* Zürich, TVZ, Theologischer Verlag, 2002.

Anselm, Reiner und Ulrich H.J. Körtner (Hg.), *Streitfall Biomedizin. Urteilsfindung in christlicher Verantwortung,* Göttingen, Vandenhoeck & Ruprecht, 2003.

Bail, Ulrike, *Körperkonzepte im Ersten Testament: Aspekte einer feministischen Antrhopologie,* Hedwig-Jahnow-Forschungsprojekt (Hrsg.), Stuttgart, Kohlhammer 2003.

Bizer, Christoph, *Die Gewalt und das Böse,* Neukirchen-Vluyn, Neukirchener Verlag, 2003.

Gruber, Franz, *Das entzauberte Geschöpf: Konturen eines christlichen Menschenbildes,* Regensburg, Pustet, 2003.

Wenzel, Knut, *Sakramentales Selbst: Der Menschen als Zeichen des Heils.* Freiburg i.Br., Herder, 2003.

Herms, Eilert, *Leben. Verständnis, Wissenschaft, Technik. Kongressband der Wissenschaftlichen Gesellschaft für Theologie,* Bd 24, Gütersloh, 2004.

Lehmkühler, Karsten, *Inhabitatio. Die Einwohnung Gottes im Menschen.* Forschungen zur Kirchen- und Dogmengeschichte, Bd. 104, Göttingen,Vandenhoeck & Ruprecht, 2004.

Matthias Zeindler, Michael Graf, Frank Mathwi (Hg.), "Was ist der Mensch?", in *Theologische Anthropologie im interdisziplinären Kontext. Wolfgang Lienemann zum 60. Geburtstag.* Forum Systematik, Bd. 22, Stuttgart, Kohlhammer, 2004.

French

Vladimir Lossky, *A l'image et à la ressemblance de Dieu,* Paris, Aubier-Montaigne, 1967.

J. Moltmann, *L'homme, Essai d'anthropologie chrétienne,* Paris, Cerf-Mame, 1979.

John Zizioulas, *L'être ecclésial. Perspectives orthodoxes*, Genève, Labor et Fides, 1981.

Adalbert G. Hamman, *L'homme, image de Dieu. Essai d'une anthropologie chrétienne dans l'Eglise des cinq premiers siècles*, Paris, Desclée, 1987.

Panayotis Nellas, *Le vivant divinise. L'anthropologie des Pères de l'Eglise*, Paris, Cerf, 1989.

Louis-Marie Chauvet, *Symbole et sacrament. Une relecture chrétienne de l'existence chrétienne*, Paris, Cerf, 1990.

Liturgie et anthropologie chrétienne: Conférences de Saint-Serge, XXXVIe Semaine d'Etudes liturgiques, Paris, 27-30 juin 1989, éditées par A.M. Traccia et A. Pistoia, Roma, C.L.V.-Edizione Liturgiche, 1990.

Edward Schillebeeckx, *L'histoire des hommes, récit de Dieu*, Paris, Cerf, 1992.

Vittorino Grassi, Luis-F. Ladaria, Philippe Lécrivain, Bernard Sesboüé, *L'homme et son salut*. Histoire des dogmes, sous la direction de Bernard Sesboüé, tome III, Paris, Desclée, 1995.

Isabelle Chareire, *Ethique et grâce. Contribution à une anthropologie chrétienne*, Paris, Cerf, 1998.

Douglas John Hall, *Etre image de Dieu: le stewardship de l'humain dans la création*, Paris, Cerf & Montréal, Bellarmin, 1998.

NOTES

NOTES